God's Boy
Copyright © 2019 by Andrew Hahn

Cover art: Daniel A. Bruce, *Pray*, 2001, neon, transformer, plywood.
        45"H x 30"W x 4"D. Courtesy of the artist.
        Photograph: Jean-Marie Guyaux

Author photograph: Tyler Carlton Williams

Cover design by Seth Pennington

Sibling Rivalry Press, LLC
PO Box 26147
Little Rock, AR 72221

info@siblingrivalrypress.com

www.siblingrivalrypress.com

ISBN: 978-1-943977-69-7

By special invitation, this title is housed in the Rare Book and Special Collections Vault of the Library of Congress.

First Sibling Rivalry Press Edition, November 2019

ANDREW HAHN

for all of God's boys at liberty university

contents

when a faggot speaks up in church

he knows what he's talking about

the preacher raises a hand to God
points to christ on the cross
says   *he didn't die so you could live this way*

the congregation claps but they won't dance
jesus didn't dance   but he didn't clap either

i want to tell them i can reach into the sky
& read the stars   like jesus in the lost
gospel of judas   & i can show them what love is
on the red constellations of my body

the preacher tells me i am going to Hell
& that he is sorry   but i know he is satisfied
i will never call church *home*   again
i will never call christians *brothers & sisters*   again
i will never sing another song of praise   again
i will never worship God in a way that reminds me of them
again

but i want to show them how to dance
i will grab jesus from the wall
& hold him in a tango
i will stick my finger into the red star on his hand

he will show me the red star dying in the sky
the rainbow dust cloud reaching the boundaries
of the burst in a halo spanning light years
& he will say   *you have made my heart explode*

it would have been easier if you died

it would have been easier if you died in the los angeles fire
i imagine a text from your friend
    idk if you heard   dan died
    we're a mess here
    let me know if we can do anything
i imagine your belongings in your friend's garage in smoke
the car you bought to save the environment blemishing the ozone

do you remember how we met

in school   in vermont   in the winter
every star in space set over the mountains
cassiopeia stitched into the navy sky
& i wanted to hold your hand bc you were perfect

for graduation six months later i gave you
the stars embroidered over vermont's green mountain
your eyes welled but you didn't cry
& i wanted to kiss you but not in front of your dad

the gift would burn w everything else in your friend's garage
    bc i know you didn't take it w you

& i know you didn't die
    but it might have been easier instead of knowing you chose to
        leave me

you're prob near a fire in india wrapped in a blanket
i hope you're looking up at the stars & thinking of me
i never want you to know that at one point
    i thought i needed you to die to keep warm

God's boy

liberty university is the world's largest evangelical university

pastor emerick told me about 2:00 a.m. phone calls from a boy
who fell in love with a man who abused him
hooked him on drugs   took him on trips &
rented him to wealthier men who   gang raped him
the man profited off the boy
the man cut him off from his family   from his friends
anyone who could save him

you don't want to be a dad/dy's boy   he said to me
you're God's boy

dad/dies call twinks *boy* in the videos i love
like the texts middle-aged men send that get me wet
    how's your day   *boy*
    come suck my dick   *boy*
    my friend is on his way   *boy*

i will fall in love with dad/dy after dad/dy who will fuck
me w intention & ask me to stay   to fasten in alignment
w his solid body   hand on my hip   the back of my neck

if only God knew how it felt to be loved by someone bigger than himself
to read a dad/dy's soul on his skin where the sun reddened his complexion
    into a story of stars
for a dad/dy to clench his wrists as he fills him w the galaxy of life

if only God knew how it felt to worship

i hate how i have your phone number memorized
i hate that i know how many raspberries you eat w breakfast
i hate how i know the title of the first poem you published
i hate how i love your favorite movie   i hate how i know
your body the way no one else does   i hate someone else will
be given the chance to love you
& maybe do it better than me

(805) 455—5xx5

the river: lynchburg

i found home
between the blue ridge & the river w a boy's name
my apartment housed the remnants of an old lover
    hanging by his wrists on the walls
    covering my mouth when i try to sleep
    i want to say so many terrible things to the men
                            who linger

when you visited   we stood at the island's edge
the city a tiered series of crumbling brick
you said   *i love ruined things*   then squeezed my hand
    & watched the brown blood from my fingertips
    sink into the soil

that night you pulled my hair
    & shoved   your fingers in my mouth
    i need you to want me this way   but you won't
    move me like that for six more months
    i am trying to remember how to miss you

i love the ways a ghost vanishes   try to feel my red & blue body
but fall through me   finally see my broken kidneys
& heart aged by grief   throw yourself into the ruined animal
cast the ruined animal into the river & see how nothing can stop you

dad/dy

▷ he wants me face down waiting for him   showered   trimmed

   (as if i would give myself to him shy of perfect)

▷ he takes me to dinner

▷ he introduces me to his friends by name

▷ he asks me on trips & pays for everything

   (w the understanding i am available to use how he pleases)

▷ he fucks me against the glass door overlooking the skyline & in
the shower & on the bed & the ottoman & kitchen counter & living
room floor & in the pool & in the car   parked in the cemetery
in someone else's backyard

   (blindfolded)

     ((for him   or his friends   or guys passing through))

       (((or for all of them at once)))

         ((((some of them call me faggot
         & say they love my wet boy pussy
         i am a boy   i am dad/dy's boy   i am just a boy))))

▷ he tells me he loves me

(he spits in my mouth   he rams his body inside mine
   he slaps my face   & leaves a mark shaped like a heart)

the atoms fastening everything together

when i touch you
i want you to believe we are more than just atoms
more than bodies of meat
my grandfather prayed hours every morning
my father collapsed to his knees in the hospital
my brother wept holding on to the dead dalmatian
i have been a body brought back to life

when i went to vermont in winter
snow dusted my growing beard
the ghost of cancer still reeking in my clothes
my car stopped working after the storm
i had to pay for laundry
i was happy

when i leave you
it won't be bc i am moving to providence
or bc i hate you
it will be bc i want you to see i am more than atoms
i will lay across you
my body shaking
like my father's shuddering over my nearly-dead body

then i took another breath

a faggot tries to be christ-like

my father said hanging by the wrists & suffocating
is necessary to be saved

in everything i did   i tried to be like christ
& christ let men in uniform
drive nails between his radius & ulna

w the way my father sometimes looks at me
i bet he would love to drive nails
into my limp faggoty wrists

was it God who tortured & hung his son on the tree
jesus begged   sweat blood
& the father said   *i'm going to kill you anyway*
was it God who whispered to the roman soldier
    to pierce jesus' side
    to spill the blood & water so something on the earth
    could be holy

does shaming & killing his son make God an angry father
does following God's teachings make fathers so cruel
is this how the church creates gods from men

i spent my whole life trying to be like jesus
but i refuse to die like him

when he penetrates me below my ribs
my father sees what i'm made of
blood & guts that have been fucked good
& the cum of men who loved me or didn't
my body hisses & deflates

i become a cloud over my own cross

my father's head turns to light
i ask him to cut himself open & show me who he is

on Hell

i am not afraid of Hell bc of the fire
fire has lit & warmed my home in the adirondacks
i learned to gather good wood for burning
to tend to the flames like a wound

i am afraid of Hell bc of the maggots in the skin
i have always been afraid of what's smaller than me
& in love w what's bigger
redwoods
the substantial body of a middle-aged man
the spirit of God

i'm afraid of Hell bc it's so permanent
i still cry over my grandfather's death 6 years ago
my father branded his hand w a red-hot hanger
i will never be held by my first love again

God created the universe in 7 days
my favorite number is 8 bc it's the number of newness
it looks like forever

if i lived in Hell for 8 days
would i forget what it felt like to feel my father's skin
soft from lotion
would i forget the human condition of a broken heart
or is that what Hell is
a heart so broken that charring skin feels like
sitting in front of the woodstove at home

dad/dy & his friends

dad/dy blindfolds me before
john arrives & pounds me hard w dad/dy in the room
    holds poppers to my nose   grunts w his chainsaw tongue
    & slaps me as he leaves for his wife

then marc afterward   the discreet bro *masc4masc*
dad/dy sits in the other room & listens to marc
hold my lips between his teeth
like he loves me   the way gay men can share intimacy
& forget it ever happened

marc lays beside me shoulder-to-shoulder
    i want him to want to get behind me & pull my hair
    to make me scream
    i want to feel him in my body tomorrow

mark is christ's disciple i forget the most   like his gospel
but i also forget the disciple who shares my name
    always in the background
    a fisher of men
    just a boy
marc has a name i want to wear
    an imprint on my body shaped the same on my tongue

he says   *you're beautiful dude*

he sounds like corona light & fantasy football
his grindr profile prob says *str8 masc dudes only*
just looking to chill maybe more

did he not use me bc he noticed my leather tote in the corner

was it the way my skinny frame may have felt like a woman's
    in his large hands
i sink in the space between the mattress & bedframe
    to hide the useless body

i say   *thanks*
he kisses me & says   *no thank you*

he passes dad/dy in the other room
& shuts the front door
i forget the sound of his voice
when dad/dy comes into the room to taste
what john & marc left behind

the best thing about having a gay brother is being erased together

the family photo shrinks from 6 to 4
your stepmom says   *there are no halves in this house*
you can't help but think your family is half-christian
bc they love you as sinners & not as their sons
they read their bibles & pray for you in private
at christmas you have no stocking   their gifts
show you how little they've tried
no one you love can enter their house
even though they say you are welcome
they don't want to make up stories to explain you
the phone calls stop coming & sometimes they don't
say   *i love you*   before hanging up
but you & your brother will talk every day
you are family
you know what it means to survive
& to love & to give & to be hurt
& to open the broken hearts you have sealed for each other w gold
even though you don't
say   *i love you*   before hanging up the phone
you know it truer than if the words dripped from God's full lips

hole in my back

there is a hole in my back
where your hand is supposed to go
the fentanyl makes me laugh
i call the bald anesthesiologist a neanderthal
& sing songs about girls
i want to sing about boys   but my dad is in the room

on my side my lumbar spreads like fingers traced on paper
this is how it would look to cuddle w you
you would hold the oxygen mask to my face
i will stop breathing after the propofol
but not breathing for a few moments is worth it to know
i am not sick anymore

reach inside the hole in my spine
& dip your hand into the
stream of clean water
i want to stand on a precipice
eye-to-eye w God   to scream   *where have you been*
for him to wash over me   to whisper   *in your blood*
& i will feel the boundary of my body when God kisses my neck
i am somewhere between the God inside me
    & the God in the air   in the trees   in you

when i wake & you try to love me
know that my chemo breath smells like my dirty blood
i might need you to feed me   to help me walk up the stairs
        to clean up my puke   to sit w me in the murk of uncertainty
when we lie down & your fingertips trace my spine
stop at the fourth vertebrae from the bottom
kiss my caved-in skin & know that
when you touch me there it hurts

boys like us

sunday i had a panic attack before going back to the church
where at 15   i learned i was Hell-bound
my faggot friend wanted to go bc he drinks too much
church makes him feel good

he doesn't know these people used to burn boys like us at the stakes
& gave us our name   bundles for burning

i am not afraid of the fire that named me
but i am afraid of what happens when hate enters the heart
& what a hateful body can do
    i have seen video clips
    of christian parents beating their sissy boys
    read articles
    of boys like us killing themselves over & over & over
    bc of church   bc of christians   bc of God

the church sanctuary is cold
it's said the presence of an evil spirit chills a room
does that mean heat summons the spirit of God

when these people set us ablaze
would they see God standing w us in the fire
like nebudchadnezzar burning the three boys

or would they be right
& God would char our skin   ashes to ashes
& break down our bones

if that's the case i'm happy to burn w someone i love
to take my friend's hand into the fire
kiss his lips   use all my tongue
& show these people how boys like us know
how to light up a room

the river: fort lauderdale

i lay w the man from the bar until shy of sunrise bc
    he held me like he loved me   he was there & you were not
    i saw the long river of tissue where he was once cut open
    he said   *they reached inside & took out the cancer*

    i want to know what it feels like to reach into a man
    & pull out the thing that hurts
    would we share something like blood   something red
    blood lovers   lips   ass   our bodies on fire w cancer

what am i looking for that i don't already have

we plunge into the intracoastal's dark water together
    two red lights in the night sky of earth
    sparking   smelling of five a.m. sex
    w his hands cupping my face bc he wants me
    he says   *i knew you were a star when i first touched you*

i want to wrap the network of my roots around his wound
    as he heals against my skin   he had given me
    everything i wanted by being here

i only have faith in what i can see

but what about the creatures underneath the river's dark waters
    that can smell the blood on our bodies &
    always have been wanting a taste

otters

did you know that when otters go to sleep
they hold hands so they won't drift apart
& sometimes they smile
i don't know why   but it's got to be
bc they make each other happy

after the last time i saw you
the sea of my twin bed somehow felt smaller
the way a body sometimes swallows stitches
i listened to the rain
against my window that december
swaddled in my sheets like kelp

& i saw in the glimmer of the street lamp
the shorts you slept in two nights ago
prostrate in the closet

i wanted nothing more than to
fall asleep to the sound of the rain
& whole notes of your breath
i wanted nothing more than to hold your hand
& smile   bc you did make me happy

now i know you wouldn't

now i know my hands can't hold a heart
that was never mine
neither can kelp
neither can shorts

the river: santa barbara

you left me to travel west in search of God
india   you said   is the holiest place in the world
    but it is the only place   outside our land   you've been

what are you looking for that you don't already have

ganga   the goddess & the river
purify & prepare the dead
    i wonder if you knew this when you dipped your hand
    into the murk   the washed sins of the nation
    now your sins   the karma from past lives
    now your karma   their wounded & dead
    now your grief

if i were a lone tree in a field in california
    would you even touch me how i want to be touched
    i want you to take my roots between your fingers
    & learn how to feed me
    i want you to dip your hand into the river of our homeland
    plunge into the earth under me   gaze
    at the network of stars in the dirt   & know
    this could be yours if you chose to stay

what i couldn't tell you

i could never tell you how often i imagined i was w someone else
bc you didn't want my body like other lovers had
my dad/dy would lay on me   not care how much it hurt me
ask me if i liked it   lock my arms in his to keep me close
he would kiss my boy mouth   tell me how much fun i am
& ask me to stay

you wouldn't have stayed if i begged you

maybe it would've been easier if i left you for the man in fort lauderdale
the one who asked me before falling asleep if
i loved you

i said yes but realized how badly i needed to say no

what made you so afraid of my body
i could see the way you shrank from your own
that someone you loved made you hate it
you touched yourself like a wound
inched away from me as you slept

on our last night together you held me
& i cried bc you were another man leaving me
& you   bc you were afraid
i never looked deep enough in your eyes
i never told you that sometimes when you touched me
i felt like i could hate me too

dad/dy & the bird

my dad/dy tried to kiss me in the morning
i said   *no stop*
he pinned my bird-bone wrists & crushed them
he flipped me on my stomach
& pulled down my pants
i said   *no stop*
my phone rang
i saw a bird flying outside the glass door
i remembered the bird that flew into my windshield
& the way its bones cracked against the machine
i remembered the way my dad/dy thought he would break me
& i said   *don't worry you won't break me*
& then he did
    bc he knew how i liked his hands

///

i could breathe again when
my dad/dy crashed to the floor against the dresser
& split open & bled on the carpet

he said   *why won't you let me love you*

i said   *i have to go*
i checked my phone & saw 50 gays were dead in orlando
& i cried on the way home
my dad/dy didn't understand why what he did was wrong
but i did
& birds soared around my car bc it was june
all of them flew beside me

dad & son

i will never be the son my father wants
    ▷ he says his life sucks now that i'm a faggot
    ▷ he says i am ungodly
    ▷ he says this could have been avoided if i played football

i'm not trying to live a perfect life
i pierced my ear   i pierced my nose
my parents believed reading vonnegut caused demonic night terrors
i went to christian university to learn how to be good
they said only God is good

after twenty years of church i pierced my hand at the altar & drank
          blood from the chalice
i will remember the son my father lost when i became a faggot
i will remember who i was before my father forgot me

what is more masc than fucking men

i think all men are born good
we are covered in our mother's blood from the beginning
we do not know sin
we know nothing but the film casing our eyes & our mother's breast
boys are not born w a bud in one hand & a dick in the other
boys are born crying

on Heaven

i don't think my parents believe my brother & i are going
    to Heaven
but sometimes   i'm not sure i want to
i want to be home somewhere
i want to be loved somewhere

can you show me where my brother will be so i
    can follow
God   i know your arms can carry me there
hold me against your skin
tell me about your boys
tell me Heaven is a place where my parents learn what
    love is

God   when you carry me to him   will you
    stay w me
will you lay me down on a bed of stars   open
    your robe
bring my hand to the red star on your chest   whisper
    when i create the new world
    i will die
    & everyone will see i've always loved you

waiting

i spent months waiting
for you to come home or for God to show up
lazarus died waiting for jesus
& it sounds the same as saying   *i would die without you*

it's hard to hear God when waiting on you
though i've felt the slow burning of a red star within me
 my father doesn't think God talks to me anymore
 bc i'm a faggot
 when my mother left him he waited weeks for her to return
 my grandmother said he was "not okay" for a long time
 but he needed to be strong for me

the only man who never made me wait was my father
you & other men have said   *i love you*
more than he ever has
i don't believe you anymore

really what i'm saying is   *i don't need you to live*
&   *i am learning to be "okay"*

but i don't hate you

i love you for reinforcing my father's love
how coming through the door & hugging me every night
is the way i imagine God devotes himself to his children
 the red star lives the longest by burning   loving   slowly
the way you promised me we would

the river: schroon lake

i drove you to the adirondacks
to stand on the lot of my burned-down childhood
i imagined how a home can be beautiful after Hell devastates it

i used to love throwing myself into the water
bc God held me somehow
i have felt the scars on his palms at the bottom of the sand
    he said   *look at the wounds i suffered bc i love you*

now i don't like being wet

i hated being baptized
    but i love how it made me part of a family
i hated drowning in the spirit
    but i love how God still works miracles

last summer in vermont i stepped in a puddle & cried
i absorbed my life on the water like thirsty soil :
    my father teaching me to water ski
    cupping minnows in my hands
    swimming at dawn
    learning how to drive a boat

when i drove you to the lot of my home
we undressed in my car
& dove in the water
i cried bc i was home   w you
& God held us in the healing pool of his hands

acknowledgments

all the sins: "when a faggot speaks up in church"
Rappahannock Review: "hole in my back"
Yes, Poetry: "a faggot tries to be christ-like"
Bending Genres: "the river: lynchburg," "dad & son"
Glass: A Journal of Poetry: "dad/dy & the bird"

A special thank you to Bethany Breitland, Melissa Lowrie, and Alexis Groulx for being the family that uplifts and supports me and for being unafraid of telling the truth even when it's hard to hear. Thank you for reading these poems and for helping me shape them and bring them to life. And a special thank you to Josiane Chriqui for the hours on the phone, the endless love, and the countless words of wisdom.

To the men who loved me or didn't, thank you for the fun. I hold our times together closely.

To my many teachers, mentors, and friends: Connie May Fowler, Richard McCann, Harrison Candelaria Fletcher, Sue William Silverman, Brian Leung, Santino DallaVecchia, Lisa Folkmire, and The Stoop Kids—I carry your words and wisdom with me always.

To TC Williams, Adam Shoaf, Derek Via, and Jack DelPriore, I have no words for how much I love you.

To Christopher Gaumer, thank you for being the first person to believe in me and to teach me writing is a way of life.

Thank you to Bryan Borland and Seth Pennington for their constant encouragement and dedication to this chapbook. I feel incredibly spoiled by you two.

And lastly, thank you to my brother Tyler Hahn, my grandmother, and my aunts Chris and Bern Pentz for their never-ending love and support. You are my everything.

To the LGBTQ+ community at Liberty University, if you feel the way my friends and I did, I promise you'll feel free soon.

the poet

Andrew Hahn is a queer poet and writer living in Fort Lauderdale.
He has his MFA from Vermont College of Fine Arts and was invited
to be the writer-in-residence at Randolph College. His poetry and
essays can be found online at *Screen Door Review*, *Butter Press*, *Crab
Fat Magazine*, *Crab Creek Review*, and *Pithead Chapel* among others.

the artist

Daniel A. Bruce was born in Altona, New York, in 1978, and works
predominately in the medium of sculpture. His education began at
Munson-Williams-Proctor Arts Institute and later at Rhode Island
School of Design, where he completed his BFA. He then earned his
MFA from Tyler School of Art in 2008. Bruce has exhibited work
at various galleries, museums, art fairs, and cultural centers in the
United States. He was an artist in residence at Sculpture Space Inc.
in Utica, New York, and also spent two summer seasons living and
working with Bread and Puppet Theater in Glover, Vermont. In
2014, he mounted a solo exhibition, in a landmarked eighteenth-
century wharf at the South Street Seaport in Manhattan, where
he explored the idiosyncrasies of folk beliefs and superstitions.
Most recently, he exhibited in Homemade at the Leslie-Lohman
Museum Project Space where he explored commonalities between
the typically marginalized spheres of folk art and gay culture. Bruce
lives and works in New York City with his husband, artist David
Mishalanie.

the press

Sibling Rivalry Press is an independent press based in Little Rock, Arkansas. It is a sponsored project of Fractured Atlas, a nonprofit arts service organization. Contributions to support the operations of Sibling Rivalry Press are tax-deductible to the extent permitted by law, and your donations will directly assist in the publication of work that disturbs and enraptures. To contribute to the publication of more books like this one, please visit our website and click *donate*.

Sibling Rivalry Press gratefully acknowledges the following donors, without whom this book would not be possible:

Tony Taylor
Mollie Lacy
Karline Tierney
Maureen Seaton
Travis Lau
Michael Broder & Indolent Books
Robert Petersen
Jennifer Armour
Alana Smoot
Paul Romero
Julie R. Enszer
Clayton Blackstock
Tess Wilmans-Higgins & Jeff Higgins
Sarah Browning
Tina Bradley
Kai Coggin
Queer Arts Arkansas
Jim Cory
Craig Cotter
Hugh Tipping
Mark Ward

Russell Bunge
Joe Pan & Brooklyn Arts Press
Carl Lavigne
Karen Hayes
J. Andrew Goodman
Diane Greene
W. Stephen Breedlove
Ed Madden
Rob Jacques
Erik Schuckers
Sugar le Fae
John Bateman
Elizabeth Ahl
Risa Denenberg
Ron Mohring & Seven Kitchens Press
Guy Choate & Argenta Reading Series
Guy Traiber
Don Cellini
John Bateman
Gustavo Hernandez
Anonymous (12)

CPSIA information can be obtained
at www.ICGtesting.com
Printed in the USA
LVHW091737301019
635835LV00007B/1053/P

9 781943 977697